I SPOT SQUARES

first concepts

BY NATALIE HUMPHREY

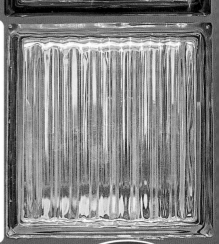

Gareth Stevens
PUBLISHING

Squares are everywhere!
The bread is a square.

3

The hat is a square.

5

The window is a square.

The soap is a square.

The pillow is a square.

The table is a square.

The game is a square.

The book is a square.

The chocolate is
a square.

19

The clock is a square.

21

Can you spot
the square?

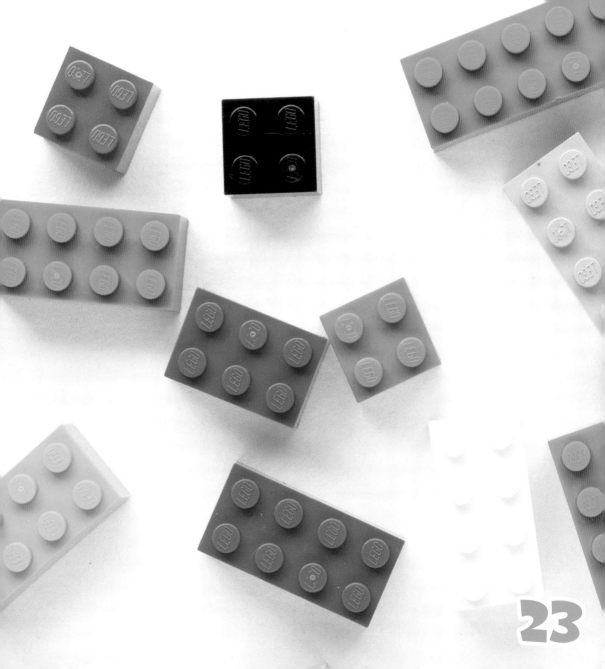

Please visit our website, www.garethstevens.com. For a free color catalog of all our high-quality books, call toll free 1-800-542-2595 or fax 1-877-542-2596.

Library of Congress Cataloging-in-Publication Data
Names: Humphrey, Natalie, author.
Title: I spot squares / Natalie Humphrey.
Description: Buffalo, New York : Gareth Stevens Publishing, [2025] |
Series: I spot shapes | Includes index.
Identifiers: LCCN 2023044273 (print) | LCCN 2023044274 (ebook) | ISBN 9781538291771 (library binding) | ISBN 9781538291764 (paperback) | ISBN 9781538291788 (ebook)
Subjects: LCSH: Square–Juvenile literature. | Shapes–Juvenile literature.
Classification: LCC QA482 .H8627 2025 (print) | LCC QA482 (ebook) | DDC 516/.154–dc23/eng/20231031
LC record available at https://lccn.loc.gov/2023044273 LC ebook record available at https://lccn.loc.gov/2023044274

Published in 2025 by
Gareth Stevens Publishing
2544 Clinton Street
West Seneca, NY 14224

Designer: Leslie Taylor
Editor: Natalie Humphrey

Photo credits: Cover edchechine/Shutterstock.com; p. 3 Yuwarin Stockphoto/Shutterstock.com; p. 5 LightField Studios/Shutterstock.com; p. 7 Ann Yuni/Shutterstock.com; p. 9 Sisacorn/ Shutterstock.com; p. 11 Melissa S Bornbach/Shutterstock.com; p. 13 Hirunya/Shutterstock.com; p. 15 LightField Studios/Shutterstock.com; p. 17 Alex Veresovich/Shutterstock.com; p. 19 IB Photography/Shutterstock.com; p. 21 koosen/Shutterstock.com; p. 23 Ev. Safronov/Shutterstock.com.

Printed in the United States of America

CPSIA compliance information: Batch #CSGS25: For further information contact Gareth Stevens, New York, New York at 1-800-542-2595.

Find us on